The Complete
FLY FISHERMAN™

FISHING NYMPHS, WET FLIES & STREAMERS

Subsurface Techniques for Trout in Streams

BY DICK STERNBERG, DAVID L. TIESZEN
& JOHN VAN VLIET

Credits

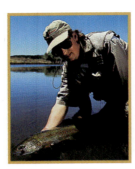

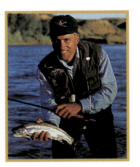

DICK STERNBERG, a longtime multispecies fly fisherman, formerly supervised the trout and salmon research program for the Minnesota DNR.

DAVID TIESZEN, a skilled flytier, has tested his patterns on trout and salmon in rivers and streams from Alaska to Argentina.

JOHN VAN VLIET is an expert fly fisherman and author of several popular books on fly fishing and tying. He also devotes his time to Trout Unlimited.

DAVE HUGHES is the well-known and widely respected author of numerous books, and is a frequent contributor to FLY FISHERMAN magazine.

COWLES
Creative Publishing

President: Iain Macfarlane
Group Director, Book Development: Zoe Graul
Creative Director: Lisa Rosenthal
Senior Managing Editor: Elaine Perry

FISHING NYMPHS, WET FLIES & STREAMERS-
Subsurface Techniques for Trout in Streams

By: Dick Sternberg, David Tieszen and John van Vliet

Executive Editor, Outdoor Group: Don Oster
Fishing Products Director and Editor: Dick Sternberg
Book Development Leader: John van Vliet
Researcher and Technical Advisor: David Tieszen
Editorial Consultants: David Hughes, John Randolph
Project Manager: Tracy Stanley
Senior Art Director: Bradley Springer
Copy Editor: Janice Cauley
Director of Photography: Mike Parker
Studio Manager: Marcia Chambers
Principal Photographers: Mike Hehner, William Lindner
Contributing Photographer: Mark Macemon
Photo Editor: Anne Price
Senior Production Manager: Gretchen Gunderson
Senior Desktop Publishing Specialist: Joe Fahey
Production Staff: Laura Hokkanen, Tom Hoops, Jeanette Moss, Mike Schauer

Illustrator: Greg Hargreaves
Travel and Location Arrangements (Argentina): Gage Outdoor Expeditions/Four Seasons Adventures – Baird Pittman, Alejandro Saint Antonin, Emilio Paris
Additional Location Assistance: Andres & Fabiana Saint Antonin, Martin & Patricia Gough, Victor Bozic

Contributing Individuals and Agencies: Tom Andersen; Dan Bailey's Fly Shop – John Bailey; Berkley; C. C. Filson Co. – Jim Rex; D. B. Dunn; G. Loomis – Bruce Holt; Hobie Outback – Bill Horner; Hobie Sunglasses – Dennis Bush; Bob Jacklin; Lefty Kreh; The Orvis Co. – Paul Ferson, Tim Joseph, Tom Rosenbauer; Ross Reels; Sage Manufacturing Corporation – Marc Bale, Don Green, David T. Low, Jr.; St. Croix Rod Company – Rich Belanger, Jeff Schluter; Scott Fly Rod Company – Todd Field, Stephen D. Phinny; Simms; 3M/Scientific Anglers – Jim Kenyon; Kurt Weineth; Bob & Lisa White

Printed on American paper by: R. R. Donnelley & Sons Co.
02 01 00 99 98 / 5 4 3 2

Copyright © 1996 by Cowles Creative Publishing, Inc.
5900 Green Oak Drive
Minnetonka, Minnesota 55343
1-800-328-3895

ISBN 0-86573-101-2

FLY FISHERMAN is a registered trademark of
Fly Fisherman magazine and is used under license.

CONTENTS

Introduction

Bring up the subject of fly fishing, and most anglers picture a trout rising to the surface to sip in a tiny dry fly. But in truth, subsurface flies account for the vast majority of fly-caught trout. *Fishing Nymphs, Wet Flies & Streamers: Subsurface Techniques for Trout in Streams*, deals only with methods for using nymphs, streamers and wet flies, the major types of subsurface patterns. Dry-fly and emerger methods are the subject of another volume in the *Complete Fly Fisherman™* series.

It's no wonder that trout respond so well to subsurface flies – they mimic immature aquatic insects, baitfish and crustaceans, foods that are present in every trout stream throughout the year. On the other hand, the adult insects that dry flies imitate are available for only brief periods.

For any subsurface technique to be effective, you must first understand the world in which trout live. The first chapter, "Understanding Trout Streams," helps you assess a stream's fishing potential by explaining how environmental factors, such as water fertility, water temperature and current speed, affect the number and size of trout a stream can produce. We also show you how to recognize the basic riffle-run-pool configuration of a trout stream and how to identify trout lies, so you'll spend your time fishing where the fish are. And we explain what trout eat and how they feed, so you'll know what type of fly to use.

The second chapter, "Subsurface Basics," shows you how trout detect danger and how to approach a potential lie without spooking the fish. Then, we give you the basic information you need for selecting and presenting each type of subsurface fly. We also show you how to handle trout properly, so you can release them to fight again.

"Subsurface Fly-Fishing Techniques," the third and final chapter, details the most effective methods for fishing trout along the bottom or in the mid-depths. You'll learn what techniques work best in what water types and how to select the right equipment for each method. Finally, using detailed step-by-step photos and diagrams, we show you how to perfectly execute each technique, including any special-purpose casts associated with it.

Trout streams come in a wide array of types, shapes and sizes, so if you limit yourself to only one or two methods, you'll fail to catch fish more often than you succeed. Studying this book and tailoring your techniques to suit the water is the first step to becoming a complete fly fisherman.

UNDERSTANDING
TROUT STREAMS

Trout Stream Habitat

Mention the term "trout stream," and most people think of flowing water that is cold, clear and unpolluted. This stereotype is accurate, but there are other requirements as well. The quantity and size of trout a stream produces depend on the factors discussed on the following pages.

Water Fertility

A stream's fertility, or level of dissolved minerals, affects the production of plankton, the fundamental link in the aquatic food

chain. Fertility depends mainly on the water source. *Limestone* streams generally have a considerably higher mineral content than *freestone* streams.

A limestone stream is normally fed by underground springs rich in calcium carbonate, an important nutrient, and flows over a streambed that supplies even more minerals. Limestone streams have more aquatic vegetation, produce more insects and crustaceans, and generally grow more and larger trout.

A freestone stream is fed by runoff or springs with a low mineral content. It typically flows over a streambed that contributes few nutrients to the water. The most productive freestone streams pick up extra nutrients from fertile tributaries. For more details on stream types, see pages 16 to 19.

Water Temperature

TEMPERATURE ZONES IN A TYPICAL TROUT STREAM

All streams that support permanent trout populations have one thing in common: a reliable source of cold water. The cold water usually comes from springs or meltwater from snow or glaciers, but in heavily forested areas it may come from water that seeps out of the soil. Streams fed by ordinary surface runoff become too warm for trout in midsummer, except in the North or at high altitudes, where air temperatures stay cool all year.

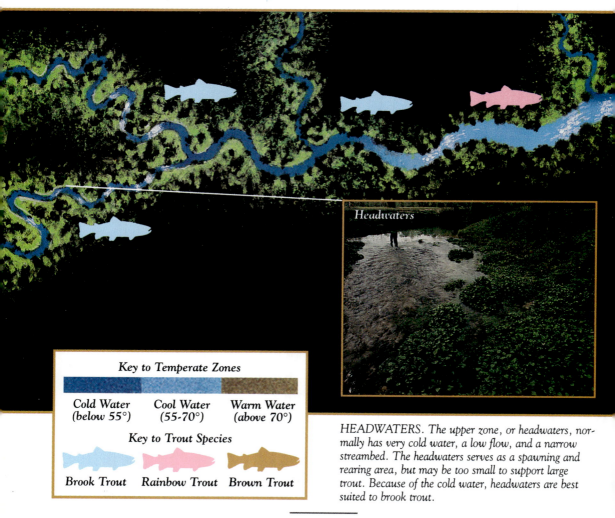

Headwaters

Key to Temperate Zones

Cold Water (below 55°)	Cool Water (55-70°)	Warm Water (above 70°)

Key to Trout Species

Brook Trout	Rainbow Trout	Brown Trout

HEADWATERS. *The upper zone, or headwaters, normally has very cold water, a low flow, and a narrow streambed. The headwaters serves as a spawning and rearing area, but may be too small to support large trout. Because of the cold water, headwaters are best suited to brook trout.*

Some trout can survive at surprisingly warm water temperatures. Browns and rainbows, for instance, live in streams where temperatures sometimes rise into the low 80s. But at these temperatures, they usually feed very little, their growth rate slows, and their resistance to disease diminishes.

The stream temperature depends not only on the water source, but also on the shape and gradient of the channel, and the amount of shade provided by streamside vegetation (pp. 12 to 13). Streams with a distinct cold-water source commonly have the temperature zones described below.

Lower zone

Middle zone

MIDDLE ZONE. *As more tributaries flow in, the stream size increases. The middle zone has cool water and is the most productive part of the stream. It has the best insect crop and generally supports the highest population of adult trout, often brooks, browns and rainbows.*

LOWER ZONE. *The stream gets even larger as more tributaries enter and the streambed flattens out. The water is warm, the current slow and the bottom silty. The lower zone supports few trout, but some of the largest ones. You may even find big browns along with suckers, carp and even catfish.*

Medium gradient (left) – moderate current, gravel-rubble bottom. Low gradient (right) – slow current, sand-silt bottom.

Gradient, Current Speed & Bottom Type

Besides affecting water temperature, the gradient, or slope, of the streambed also influences current speed and bottom composition. The higher the gradient, the faster the current and the larger the particles that the current will carry.

The most productive trout streams have a medium gradient, ranging from .5 to 2 percent, which converts to a drop of 25 to 100 feet per stream mile. Such a stream usually has moderate current and a gravel-rubble bottom, which produces an abundance of insect life and provides a good spawning substrate.

Mountain streams may have a much higher gradient, sometimes as great as 15 percent. Above 7 percent, a stream must have stairstep pools, pocket water (p. 27), log jams or other slack-water areas if it is to support trout. Otherwise, the current would be too swift.

If a stream has a gradient of less than .5 percent, the water is likely to be too warm for trout and the current may not be strong enough to wash away silt that enters the stream from nearby farm fields, logging operations and overgrazed or otherwise eroded streambanks. Silt fills the spaces between the gravel, destroying insect habitat and causing eggs deposited in the gravel to suffocate. Conservation agencies attempt to reduce siltation by fencing trout streams to keep out cattle, thereby allowing streambank vegetation to redevelop.

Shade

Most streams require some shade from trees or overhanging grasses to keep the water cool enough for trout. A stream that lacks sufficient shade will be cool enough in the upper reaches, but the water will warm rapidly as it moves downstream, so the trout zone is limited. A stream with too much shade may hold trout over most of its length, but the cold temperature and lack of sunlight inhibit food production and slow trout growth. Fisheries managers have found that they can maximize trout production by planting or removing trees to regulate the amount of shade.

Shape of Stream Channel

The shape of the stream channel affects a stream's water temperature, current speed and habitat diversity. A narrow, deep channel is generally best. In a wide, shallow one, a higher percentage of the water is exposed to the air and sun, causing the water to warm more rapidly.

Where the channel is too wide, there is not enough current to keep silt in suspension. So it settles out, smothering gravel beds that provide food and spawning habitat. Stream-improvement projects are often intended to narrow a channel that has been widened by eroding banks or beaver dams.

Streams that meander have more diverse habitat than streams with a straight channel and, consequently, have more natural cover for trout. As a stream winds along, banks along the outside bends become undercut and tree roots wash out, making ideal hiding spots. Where habitat is varied, so is the food supply. Many types of aquatic insects thrive in riffles and runs; baitfish and burrowing aquatic insects abound in pools. If a stream has aquatic vegetation, like stonewort or watercress, the plants often host scuds, midge larvae and other trout foods. Diverse habitat also provides plenty of resting and spawning areas.

When the channel is artificially straightened, riffle-run-pool habitat disappears, and so do the trout.

Meandering streams (left) have diverse trout habitat; channelized streams (right), uniform habitat.

Stability of Flow

Almost any stream can support trout in spring, when water temperatures are cool and flows are high. But trout must live in the stream year-around. If the flow falls too low, even for a few days, trout will probably not survive.

Low flows present the biggest problem in late summer, especially in areas with little forest cover to preserve ground moisture. If the weather is hot and there has been little rain, too much water evaporates from the stream, reducing the depth and slowing the current so the remaining water warms faster. Even if trout survive the warm water, they are under so much stress that they do not feed.

Low water can also be a problem in winter. In a dry year, winter flows may drop so low that the stream freezes to the bottom.

Large underground springs provide the most stability. They ensure at least a minimal flow so the stream doesn't dry up during a drought. And because spring water comes out of the ground at the same temperature year-around, these streams stay cool in summer and relatively warm in winter.

Clarity, Dissolved Oxygen & pH

Most trout species prefer clear water, although some, like browns and rainbows, can tolerate low clarity. Clear water allows sunlight to penetrate to the streambed, promoting the growth of plants, which, in turn, produce trout food. Clear water also makes it easy for trout to see food and avoid predators, including fishermen.

A lack of adequate dissolved oxygen is rarely a problem in trout streams, unless the water is quite stagnant and high in organic pollutants. In most instances, oxygen is replenished through contact with the air.

In most streams the exact pH level is of little importance to fishermen. Trout, like most fish, can tolerate a wide range of pH levels, and can live in waters with a pH as low as 4.5 or as high as 9.5. But acidic water limits food production in streams near the low end of this pH spectrum, limiting trout production. Extremely low pH levels resulting from acid rain have wiped out brook trout in parts of the Northeast.

HABITAT PREFERENCES OF TROUT

Species	Water Temp. (°F)	Current Speed	Other
Rainbow trout	55-60°	medium-fast	Often strays far from cover to find food. Commonly holds and feeds in fast riffles and pocket water that other trout species avoid.
Brown trout	60-65°	slow-medium	Most cover-oriented of all trout. Often holds tight to cover during the day, then comes out to feed at night.
Brook trout	52-56°	medium	Commonly found in cold headwaters. Intolerant of pollution.
Cutthroat trout	55-62°	medium	Thrives in inaccessible waters, particularly in the West. Because they often live in food-poor waters, they eagerly take flies and are considered "stupid."
Bull trout	45-55°	medium	Found in deep holes of large western streams. Populations have declined in many areas due to improper logging and agricultural practices.
Dolly Varden	50-55°	medium	Prefers deep pocket water in coastal streams. Also found in cold streams in mountainous areas.
Arctic char	45-50°	fast	Sea-run fish enter streams from Alaska across the Arctic coast to spawn in late summer.
Arctic grayling	42-50°	medium	Found along edges of fast current in clear, cold, unpolluted waters of large rivers and rocky creeks in the Far North or at high altitudes.

Common Types of Trout Streams

Trout can be found in streams ranging in size from meadow brooks narrow enough to hop across, to major rivers large enough to carry oceangoing vessels. Described below are the most common types of trout streams, representing both the limestone and freestone categories.

FREESTONE STREAMS

MEDIUM-GRADIENT FREESTONE STREAMS, the most common trout stream type, have moderate current with numerous pools, riffles and runs. The streambed is comprised mostly of large gravel, rubble and boulders, and has some pocket water (p. 27). These streams are fed mainly by surface runoff and meltwater.

Because the water carries few nutrients, these streams are relatively unproductive. But many have large tributary systems that add enough nutrients to produce abundant food and large trout. The best of these streams have many springs and clean, rocky bottoms that provide habitat for aquatic insects.

HIGH-GRADIENT FREESTONE STREAMS, *fed mainly by snowmelt and surface runoff, are usually found in mountainous areas. The current is fast, with long stretches of pocket water but few pools. Because of the limited food supply, trout usually run small but are willing biters.*

LOW-GRADIENT FREESTONE *streams wind through bogs, meadows or woodlands. They have sandy or silty bottoms, and undercut banks or deadfalls for cover. Some streams, fed by springs or meltwater, have clear water; others, fed by swamp drainage, have tea-colored water.*

LIMESTONE:

• *high content of minerals, particularly calcium carbonate*

• *abundant aquatic vegetation*

• *abundant year-round crop of aquatic insects and crustaceans*

• *high trout production*

FREESTONE:

• *low mineral content*

• *sparse aquatic vegetation*

• *trout foods may be scarce at some times of the year*

• *low to moderate trout production*

LIMESTONE STREAMS

LOW-GRADIENT LIMESTONE *streams have some springwater flow, move slowly, and have a meandering stream-bed composed of silt, sand or small gravel. The depth is fairly uni-form, with few riffles. In meadow streams, a common variety, over-hanging grass is the primary cover for trout.*

MEDIUM-GRADIENT LIMESTONE streams normally have some spring flow, moderate to fast current, a riffle-run-pool configuration, and a streambed composed of gravel, rubble or boulders. Many such streams flow over exposed limestone bedrock and have large populations of insects and crustaceans.

OTHER TYPES OF TROUT STREAMS

TAILWATER STREAMS, fed by cold water from the depths of a reservoir, often hold large trout populations, including many fish of trophy size. The best tailwater streams have stable flows, allowing development of rooted vegetation that holds many aquatic insects. Trout are not as numerous in tailwater streams where the water level fluctuates greatly as water is released to drive power turbines. These fluctuations limit insect populations and trout reproduction.

SPRING CREEKS arise from groundwater sources. They have slow to moderate current and very clear water. The stable water level allows development of lush weed growth, resulting in heavy insect populations. Some spring creeks produce tremendous numbers of crustaceans and surprisingly large trout.

The Mechanics
of Moving Water

Why does a trout lie upstream of a boulder when there is a noticeable eddy on the downstream side? Why does it choose a feeding lie on the bottom when most of its food is drifting on the surface? And why does a fly cast near the bank drift more slowly than the fly line in midstream?

Questions like these have a direct bearing on your ability to find and catch trout. Answering them correctly requires a basic understanding of stream hydraulics. The trout holds on the upstream side of the boulder because an eddy forms upstream of an object as well as downstream. The trout chooses a feeding lie on the bottom because friction with bottom materials slows the current to as little as one-fourth the speed in the center of the stream (below). Similarly, the fly next to the bank drifts more slowly than the fly line because friction with the bank slows the current.

BASIC STREAM HYDRAULICS

CURRENT SPEED varies within the stream cross section. The blue area has slow current; the purple, moderate current; the red, fast current. Water in the fast zone moves up to four times as fast as that in the slow zone. For purposes of illustration, the fast zone is depicted in the middle of the stream, but it could occur in any part of the stream's cross section, depending on the shape of the channel.

EDDIES form both upstream and downstream of a boulder. Many anglers do not realize that there is an eddy on the upstream side; they work only the downstream eddy, bypassing a lot of trout. Eddies also form downstream of points, sharp bends, islands and obstacles such as bridge pilings.

PLUNGE POOLS form at the base of a falls as a result of the cascading water. Plunge-pool depth may exceed the distance from the crest of the falls to the water level. A dugout often forms at the base of the falls, making one of the best trout feeding and resting lies in the stream, especially for large trout.

UNDERCUTS occur in meandering streams because current flowing to the outside of a bend becomes swifter, eroding the streambank. At the same time, current on the opposite side of the stream slackens, depositing sediment and forming a bar or point. In almost all cases, the outside bends and eddies below the bars and points hold the most trout.

Stream Habitat Types

THE RIFFLE-RUN-POOL SEQUENCE

Understanding how moving water shapes the stream channel and learning to recognize the resulting habitat types improves your chances of finding trout. In most good trout streams, the current creates a riffle-run-pool sequence that repeats itself along the stream course. The sequence may not be as noticeable in very large streams or streams with a very slow current, but the pattern is usually there.

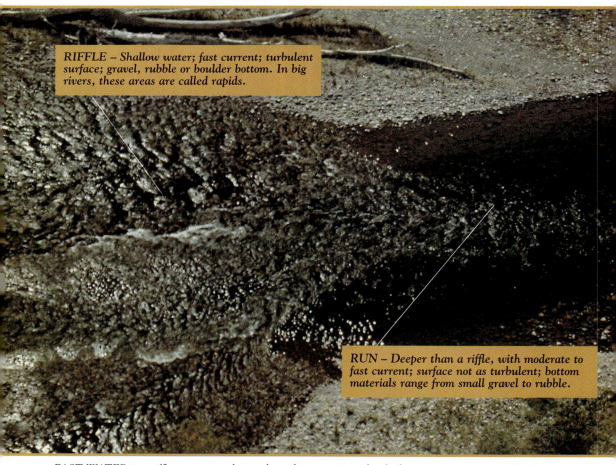

RIFFLE – Shallow water; fast current; turbulent surface; gravel, rubble or boulder bottom. In big rivers, these areas are called rapids.

RUN – Deeper than a riffle, with moderate to fast current; surface not as turbulent; bottom materials range from small gravel to rubble.

FAST WATER in a riffle excavates a deeper channel, or run, immediately downstream. As current digs the run deeper, the velocity slows, forming a pool. Because of the slower current, sediment is deposited at the pool's downstream

Besides the basic riffle, run and pool habitats, most trout streams have other important kinds of water, such as flats, undercut banks and pocket water.

With a little practice, most of these habitat types are easy to recognize, but some, such as undercut banks, may not be readily apparent.

A deep, stagnant pool may hold several good-size brown trout, but rainbows and brook trout are more likely to be found in the faster water of a run. Unless they have some pocket water, riffles hold only small trout during most of the day, but they are important feeding areas. Larger trout move into them in low-light periods, whenever a hatch is in progress or when drifting insects are abundant.

POOL – *Deep, slow-moving water with a flat surface; bottom of silt, sand or small gravel. Similar but shallower areas are called flats.*

end, raising the streambed and channeling the water into a smaller area. With the flow more constricted, the current speeds up, forming another riffle. The sequence then repeats.

Trout Lies

T rout take up positions, or *lies*, in moving water based on the way it meets a set of three basic needs. The first need is shelter from constant current. Trout cannot swim against a strong current all day any more than you can run uphill all day. They rest behind objects that break the current; otherwise, they would soon tire. But they hold close enough to the current so they can dash out and intercept any food it delivers.

The second need is protection from predators. Trout prefer water that is rough enough or deep enough that predatory birds, such as kingfishers and ospreys, cannot see them on the bottom. They hold where some type of cover, such as a log, undercut bank or deep pool, lets them escape pursuit by other predators.

Small and even medium-size trout may risk predation by feeding in shallow water, far from any shelter. But you'll seldom find large trout feeding in the shallows, unless there is some cover that they can easily reach.

The third need is adequate food. This need often overrides the other two. Trout live by a simple formula: the food they eat must provide more energy than they expend getting it. Trout will fight a strong current if hatching, migrating or drifting insects suddenly offer enough food to justify the extra energy required. During a heavy hatch, they may hold near the surface of a pool or flat and feed greedily, exposing themselves to overhead predation.

These three needs prompt trout to hold in certain water types, and avoid others. Whenever you look at a stretch of water and wonder where to start fishing, ask yourself, "Where does the water best meet one, two or even all three of these basic needs?" That's where you'll find fish.

The photos on the following pages show you some examples of each of the basic types of trout lies.

READING THE WATER

An experienced stream fisherman can learn a great deal about a stream simply by walking its banks and "reading" the water. He observes current patterns, surface disturbances, coloration differences, changes in bottom type, and other clues that reveal the hiding spots of trout.

Current patterns pinpoint the location of rocks, logs or other underwater objects that shelter the fish from the moving water. Current pushing against a bank may indicate an undercut that offers cover. The seam between fast and slow current makes a good feeding station; trout hold in the slower water waiting for food to drift by in the faster water.

Novice stream fishermen often pass up any water where the surface is broken and ripply, mistakenly assuming it is too fast and shallow for trout. But if you look carefully, this water may have slack-water pockets. A small pocket behind a rock might be home to a good-size trout, even though the water is only a foot deep.

Bottom makeup also dictates where trout will be found. A section of stream with a sandy bottom generally supports fewer trout than a section with a rocky or gravelly bottom. Important trout foods, especially larval aquatic insects, thrive among rocks and gravel, but may be completely absent in sand.

If possible, examine the stream from a high angle to get an idea of streambed contour and location of boulders, submerged logs, weed patches and other underwater objects. You can see most on a bright day when the sun is at its highest. Polarized sunglasses will remove the glare so you can see into the water.

Holding Lies

These are the most common kinds of lies. Trout find shelter from current and protection from predators in a holding lie, but usually not enough food to sustain themselves. Holding lies can be found wherever the water is deeper than three to four feet and has some sort of obstruction to break the current. Find a spot like this and you'll nearly always find one or two trout in it. They'll be feeding opportunistically, taking whatever the current delivers to them. If you drift a submerged nymph or retrieve a wet fly or streamer past them, they'll most likely take it.

TYPES OF HOLDING LIES

DEEP HOLES *appear as dark areas in the streambed. Trout move into holes to escape the current. The best holes have boulders or logs for cover.*

EDDIES below points create slackwater pools where trout can escape the current. Some such eddies form reverse-current pools that hold many trout.

UPWELLING SPRINGS appear as light spots of bubbling sand where the silt has been washed away. Because of their stable temperature, they draw trout in summer and winter.

Feeding Lies

I n these lies, trout find plenty of aquatic insects drifting along the bottom or swimming toward the surface for emergence, or they may find adult insects that fall into the water and drown. Some feeding lies provide a source of minnows, sculpins or crayfish. A feeding lie offers food to the trout, but at the expense of energy to fight the current and increased risk of predation. Trout leave a holding lie to move onto a nearby feeding lie only when enough food becomes available to justify the switch. When the food disappears, they'll move back to the holding lie.

TYPES OF FEEDING LIES

POCKET WATER is relatively shallow, with scattered boulders. It may appear too shallow, but the pockets and slots around the boulders often hold feeding trout.

CURRENT SEAMS make good feeding lies; trout hold in the slower water at the edge of a seam and pick off drifting insects.

TYPES OF FEEDING LIES *(cont.)*

WEED PATCHES hold trout because they harbor aquatic insects and crustaceans. The patches may be difficult to see, especially in low light. But the weeds usually slow the current enough to create slick spots on the surface.

OVERHANGING BRUSH collects grasshoppers and other terrestrial insects, which fall into the water and become trout food. The brush also furnishes shade and overhead protection.

RIFFLES draw trout around dusk and dawn, when the most larval insects are drifting. Deep riffles may hold some trout in midday, as well.

TAILOUTS of pools make ideal feeding stations, because the funneling effect carries drifting insects to the waiting trout.

Prime Lies

These are the best but least common lies. All three needs of trout are met in one place. They find shelter from the current, protection from predators and a constant supply of food. The largest trout in any stretch of stream will be found in its prime lies. Often a prime lie holds one big trout, which nestles into the most advantageous spot, and several smaller trout, which assume less desirable positions.

TYPES OF PRIME LIES

UNDERCUT BANKS can be found by watching the current. If it is angling toward a bank, rather than flowing parallel to it, the bank is undercut. Undercuts provide shade and overhead protection from predators and are magnets for baitfish.

PLUNGE POOLS may hold several large trout. The fish can take cover and rest in the deep eddy at the base of the falls and let the current deliver food to them.

DEEP RUNS, just downstream from riffles, rank among the top prime lies. Trout feed on nymphs and larvae washed in from the riffle above.

BOULDERS provide shade and shelter from the current, yet trout can easily dart out to grab drifting insects and quickly return to cover. You can find boulders and other underwater obstructions by looking for the boil that forms just downstream when current deflects upward. Remember that the boil forms downstream of the boulder, so you must cast upstream of the boil.

BRUSH PILES break the current, draw minnows and offer overhead protection, so they make excellent lies for good-size trout.

ROOT-WADS of fallen trees often have scour holes beneath them, furnishing superb trout cover with easy access to drifting food.

Empty Water

The majority of the water in a typical trout stream has no productive trout lies. It simply fails to meet any of a trout's needs. It's important to recognize this empty water, so you won't waste time fishing it. Empty water may be just inches deep and very fast, with nothing to obstruct the current. Or, it could be slow and featureless, with a silty bottom that harbors no trout food and offers no cover.

TYPES OF EMPTY WATER

SHALLOW RIFFLES, only a few inches deep, may draw trout at spawning time, but lack the depth to hold trout at other times.

STAGNANT POOLS have no noticeable current and a very smooth, featureless, silty bottom. They often hold large numbers of roughfish, but very few trout.

FEATURELESS FLATS have no boulders to create the pockets needed for trout cover. Trout would be easy prey for birds in the smooth, shallow water.

HEWITT RAMPS, used mainly on high-gradient streams, function much like small dams. A deeper pool forms above the structure; a scour hole below.

Common Stream-Improvement Devices

BOULDERS are sometimes placed in featureless streambeds to create trout habitat.

Many trout streams have been damaged by erosion, beaver activity, channelization or logging. Natural resources agencies, conservation groups and sportsmen's clubs sometimes reclaim these streams by installing devices to deepen the channel and provide good cover for trout.

Stream-improvement structures may be difficult to see because fisheries managers take great pains to make them look natural. The trick to fishing a reclaimed stream is simply learning to recognize the various structures and understanding how they work. Then, you can use the fishing techniques that would work in similar natural cover. Shown on these pages are the most common stream-improvement devices.

DEFLECTORS, made of rocks or logs, are used to direct water toward the opposite bank, creating undercuts that make ideal trout cover. Often, they are used in conjunction with crib shelters (below).

CRIB SHELTERS, man-made undercuts supported by pilings, are built along outside bends. Water is directed toward the structure by a deflector on the opposite bank, keeping the undercut scoured out. The photo at left shows the shelter under construction; the photo above, a year later.

Trout Foods

In the first few years of their life, trout feed heavily on immature forms of aquatic insects and, to a lesser extent, on adult insects, both aquatic and terrestrial. Other common foods include earthworms, leeches, mollusks and small crustaceans, particularly scuds. But as trout grow larger, their food habits change. While they continue to consume all of these foods, bigger food items, such as small fish and crayfish, make up an increasing percentage of their diet.

Much has been written about the highly selective feeding habits of trout. But in reality, they feed nonselectively most of the time. Like most other predatory game-fish, trout are opportunists, taking whatever foods are available at the moment.

The tendency to feed nonselectively is greatest when trout are feeding beneath the surface. Then, they'll take most any invertebrate the current delivers. Ideally, it would be best to match the size of your flies to the size of the naturals in the stream, but if you're not sure, use flies in sizes 14 or 16; these match up well with the majority of trout foods in most streams. Nearly all trout foods blend in with the bottom, so it pays to select flies in natural colors, such as green, tan or brown.

During a heavy insect hatch, however, trout may feed very selectively, ignoring everything but a certain insect form. To most trout fishermen, selective feeding means that the fish are taking a specific insect on the surface. But in many cases, trout take the insects just as they rise from the bottom, requiring anglers to use subsurface techniques. When trout are feeding selectively, you don't have to match the hatch precisely, but you must imitate the

size, shape and color of the natural more closely than you do when the fish are feeding nonselectively.

The Stream Food Primer that follows shows the most common foods and a selection of flies that resemble them.

The way trout feed and the foods they prefer vary considerably among different trout species. The Trout Diet and Feeding Habits chart on page 42 will help you link the foods to the fish. Techniques for checking food availability in the waters you fish are shown on page 43.

Mayfly (Ephemeroptera) Nymphs and their Imitations

SWIMMER NYMPHS *are long and streamlined, built for flitting through the water. They swim in short bursts and have 2 or 3 tails. These small nymphs prefer slow current and are most numerous in spring creeks, limestone streams and tailwaters. Use a size 14 to 18 fly.*

Blue-wing Olive Nymph

Swimmer

Dark Hendrickson Nymph

Crawler

CRAWLER NYMPHS *are robust and blocky, with heavy legs and 3 tails. They crawl around on bottom rocks, or in aquatic vegetation, but do not swim well. They adapt to a wide range of stream types, from rocky freestone streams to weedy spring creeks. Use size 12 to 16 flies.*

CLINGER NYMPHS have flat bodies for hugging rocks in the fast current of freestone streams. The head is wider than the body; the legs, wide and flat. They have 2 or 3 tails. Although they usually live in violent riffles or pocket water, they migrate to quieter water to hatch. Use size 10 to 16 flies.

Clinger

Jacklin's March Brown Nymph

Burrower

Hexagenia Nymph

BURROWING NYMPHS have 3 tails, and may be more than 2 inches long. Some species have large gills that ripple in waves down their backs and give them an enticing action when they swim. Because they are burrowers, they live only in slower water where the bottom is composed of silt, mud, clay and, occasionally, gravel of pea size or smaller. Use size 4 to 10 flies.

STONEFLY (PLECOPTERA) NYMPHS AND THEIR IMITATIONS

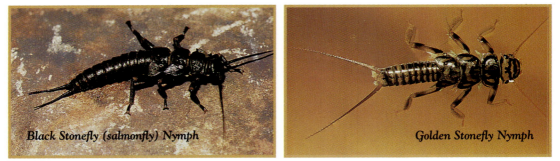

Black Stonefly (salmonfly) Nymph

Golden Stonefly Nymph

STONEFLY NYMPHS *live in cold, clean, rocky, fast-moving streams throughout North America. The most important ones are ½ to 1½ inches long, although salmonflies, found in the West, may be 2 inches in length. Stonefly nymphs have 2 pairs of wingpads, 2 antennae, 2 tail filaments and gills on the underside of the thorax. Most stonefly nymphs are black to chocolate brown, but some, called golden stoneflies, may be golden yellow with distinctive markings on the head and thorax. Use weighted nymphs in sizes 2 to 16.*

Giant Black Stonefly Nymph

Golden Stonefly Nymph

MIDGE (DIPTERA) LARVAE AND PUPAE AND THEIR IMITATIONS

Midge Larva

**Marabou
Midge
Larva**

Brassie

Midge Pupa

MIDGE LARVAE AND PUPAE *are very small but important, because they are abundant in most trout waters, especially spring creeks and tailwaters. They usually live in silty bottoms or in rooted vegetation. The larvae are thinner than caddis larvae and vary widely in color. You rarely need to use an exact imitation, because trout seldom feed selectively on them. The pupae, which have a bulge of developing wings and legs, are usually some shade of black, tan, olive or brown. Trout may feed selectively on them during a hatch and are more likely to take emerging pupae than adults on the surface. Use imitations in sizes 14 through 24.*

CADDISFLY (TRICHOPTERA) LARVAE AND THEIR IMITATIONS

Case-building Caddis Larva

Free-living Larva

CADDISFLIES can tolerate warmer water and lower oxygen levels than mayflies or stoneflies and are found in a wider variety of water types. Case-building larvae live in stick or stone cases, usually attached to the bottom of rocks. Free-living types, such as green rock worms (above, right), crawl though the spaces between stones in riffles, capturing and eating larvae of other insects. Some caddis larvae, called net spinners, weave a "gill net" that collects food particles from the current. Others, called tube makers, dig a tunnel in the bottom. All of these larvae are wormlike, lacking wingpads and tails. They vary in color from tan to bright green. Use flies in sizes 10 to 16.

Peeking Caddis

Peacock Larva

Caddis Pupa

Caddis Pupa

CADDISFLY PUPAE are the intermediate stage between the larvae and the adult. They differ from the larvae in that their legs and wings are more developed. The pupae cut their way out of their larval case and swim or float to the surface, usually in riffles or runs. Trout feed more heavily on the pupae than the larvae because they're easier to find and capture. The pupae are usually cream, tan, brown, olive or orange and are best imitated with flies in sizes 10 to 16.

MINNOWS AND THEIR IMITATIONS

Chub

Dace

Shiner

MINNOWS commonly eaten by trout include chubs, dace and shiners. Trout prefer minnows from 1 to 3 inches long, but big trout will eat much larger ones. Minnows live in all types of habitat, but most are found in fairly slow water in deep runs and pools. Bright-colored streamers in sizes 4 through 10 make the best minnow imitations and are usually fished in the same type of water. Around dusk and dawn, however, streamers work well for trout feeding in riffles or other shallow water.

Mickey Finn

Black-nosed Dace

Gray Ghost

OTHER BAITFISH AND THEIR IMITATIONS

Darter

Madtom

Sculpin

OTHER BAITFISH favored by trout include sculpins, darters and madtoms. These baitfish are usually found on clean, rocky bottoms, where they take cover around or beneath rocks. Dark- or natural-colored muddler- or matuka-type patterns in sizes 4 to 10 make good imitations; fish them across the tailout of a pool at dawn or dusk, and even at night.

Black Marabou Muddler

Black Matuka

Olive Whit's Sculpin

OTHER COMMON TROUT FOODS AND THEIR IMITATIONS

Scud

SCUDS are crustaceans, more closely related to crayfish than to aquatic insects. But they share the slow-water habitat preferred by mayfly swimmer nymphs, and are often found around weeds. They are most abundant in spring creeks and tailwaters. They swim along lazily with brisk movements of their many swimmer legs, and use their tails to dart backward. Most scuds are olive, gray, tan, pinkish or orangish, and can be imitated with size 12 and 18 nymphs.

Pink Scud

Crayfish

Clouser's Crayfish

CRAYFISH are a favorite of large trout. Found in most types of trout water, they are most numerous on rubble or weedy bottoms with slow to moderate current. They have 5 sets of legs, with the first set being greatly enlarged to form claws, or pincers. Their strong, flexible tail propels them backward very rapidly. Crayfish vary widely in color from dark brown to olive to reddish to bluish. Imitate them with size 4 to 8 flies.

Leech

Woolly Bugger

LEECHES have a slow, snakelike swimming motion that is irresistible to trout. When not feeding, leeches cling to rocks or sticks on the bottom or attach themselves to rooted vegetation in areas with slow current. Marabou patterns, such as Woolly Buggers, in black, brown, gray or olive, make good leech imitations because the material has an undulating action in the water. Natural leeches vary from 1 to 4 inches long; imitations are usually tied for the middle of that range, on size 4 to 12 hooks.

TROUT DIET AND FEEDING HABITS

Species	Common Foods	Feeding Habits
Rainbow trout	Mainly immature aquatic insects, also plankton, fish eggs, small fish, crustaceans.	Normally feeds on the bottom, but may take hatching insects on the surface.
Brown trout	Primarily immature and adult aquatic insects and terrestrial insects; large browns prefer fish and crayfish.	Feeds most heavily around dusk and dawn and at night. Prone to surface feeding.
Brook trout	Immature and adult aquatic insects, terrestrial insects and small fish; diet extremely varied.	Not as selective as most other trout. High summer water temperatures may slow feeding.
Golden trout	Insects, especially caddisfly and midge larvae; also tiny crustaceans.	Eats smaller food items than do most other trout.
Cutthroat trout	Immature and adult aquatic insects, small fish, fish eggs, crustaceans.	One of the least selective and easiest to catch of all trout.
Bull trout	Mostly fish; also immature aquatic insects, mollusks, crustaceans.	Usually feeds beneath the surface.
Dolly Varden	Mainly small fish and fish eggs; also immature aquatic insects.	Commonly eats free-drifting eggs of migrating salmon in fall.
Arctic char	Small fish, fish eggs, insects, freshwater clams, small crustaceans, plankton.	Because they live in such a stark environment, they feed on whatever foods are available.
Arctic grayling	Mainly terrestrial insects and fish eggs; also aquatic insects, small fish, mollusks, crustaceans.	Often seen dappling the surface for terrestrial insects.

Checking Food Availability

In order to select the best fly, you must know what insects the trout are eating. There is no need to identify the exact species of insect, but you must determine the size, shape and color. You could find out by checking the stomach contents of a trout, but that means you first have to catch one and, in checking, you will probably kill the fish. Following are some ways to determine food availability without checking stomachs.

SEINING *is best done with a piece of screen or fine-mesh netting stretched between two sticks. Stand upstream of the seine and shuffle your feet to dislodge insects and other bottom organisms, which then drift into the net.*

PICK UP ROCKS *and check them for clinging insects, such as caddisfly larvae and stonefly nymphs.*

CHECK CLUMPS *of weeds for aquatic insect larvae and scuds.*

SUBSURFACE
BASICS

Getting Started

Before you learn the basic methods for fishing subsurface flies, you must know how to approach trout and how to get into the best position for making a cast without spooking them.

Trout depend mainly on vision to detect danger, but they also have a well-developed lateral-line sense and an excellent sense of smell. Experienced stream fishermen know that a shadow, a sudden movement, a heavy footstep or a fly rod glinting in the sunlight will send a trout scurrying for cover. When any of a trout's sensory alarms are tripped, it's not likely to take a fly for a while. We'll show you how to minimize the chances that a trout will detect you.

You should also understand the three major types of subsurface fishing: nymphing, streamer fishing and wet-fly fishing. This chapter explains the merits of each, tells you when and where they work best, and gives you some guidelines on using them.

Finally, we'll show you how to properly handle and release trout, to minimize the chances of injuring them.

WEAR clothing that blends in with your surroundings. Drab colors, such as tan or green, are less likely to spook trout than bright colors.

Approaching Trout

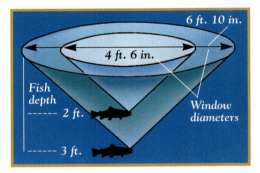

THE WINDOW is the round area on the surface through which fish view the outside world. The window's diameter is about twice the trout's depth. Surrounding the window is a mirror, through which the fish cannot see.

M̲ost stream fishermen believe that they can approach trout undetected if they just stay low and keep out of the trout's window of vision (below). But because of the way light rays are refracted by water, trout can actually "see around corners" (opposite). Even when it appears that the bank is concealing you, trout may be able to see you. Consequently, you'll have to stay lower than you thought, or stay behind streamside vegetation, to avoid detection. It also pays to keep your fly rod as low as possible.

Wading waves can also reveal your presence, so if you have a choice, always approach trout by wading upstream. Not only does the current keep the wading waves from getting to the trout, it also prevents any bottom debris you kick up from washing over them.

Common sense dictates staying in the shadows and wearing drab-colored clothing, but anglers sometimes forget to wear a drab-colored hat. That can be a big mistake, because a hat is the item of clothing most likely to be seen by trout.

TIPS FOR APPROACHING TROUT

STAY in shadows whenever possible. This way, trout are less likely to make out your form, and they won't catch a glint of sunlight off your rod or reel.

AVOID making wading waves. They can put trout down in a hurry, especially in smooth or slow-moving water, or when you're wading downstream. In fast or choppy water, the waves are not as noticeable. If you wade upstream, the current prevents the waves from reaching the fish.

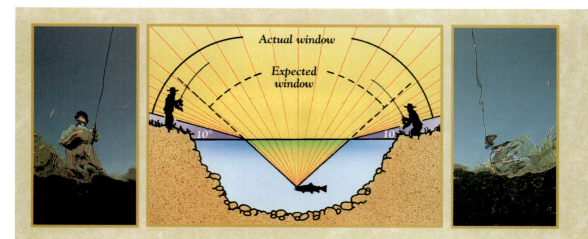

HOW TROUT VIEW THE OUTSIDE WORLD

LIGHT RAYS entering the water vertically are not bent at all, so trout clearly see objects directly above them. Rays entering the water at an angle are bent; the lower the angle, the more the bending. Because of this bending, the actual window is much wider than the expected window. Although both anglers in this diagram are out of the expected window, the trout can still see them. The angler on the left, however, is more clearly visible than the one on the right, because the light rays striking him are not bent as much. To get completely out of the trout's window, you would have to stay in the purple zone, at an angle of about 10° above the water's surface. If you're 40 feet from the edge of the window, you can stand up without being seen; at 20 feet, you would have to kneel.

Nymphing Basics

Nymphing is arguably the most consistently productive method of taking trout on flies. No matter how low or high a stream may be, no matter how cold or warm, the naturals that nymphs imitate are always present and available to the trout.

In fly fishing, the term *nymph* is used quite loosely. Nymphs may imitate natural insect nymphs, larvae or pupae, or other foods, such as scuds. When an angler is "nymphing," he may be using flies that imitate any of these food types.

Some nymphs are close imitations of particular species, as exact as flytiers can make them. Others are impressionistic, meant to suggest a variety of naturals in shape, size and coloration. Many nymphs have bodies that are thick at the front and thinner at the rear, simulating the wing pads and abdomen of the real thing. Often, there's soft, sparse hackle or picked-out dubbing to serve as legs.

A nymph pattern may be tied in weighted and unweighted versions. Weighted nymphs have a metal bead head or lead or copper wire wound onto the hook shank under the body material. They are used for fishing near bottom, especially in fast current. Unweighted nymphs work well for fishing shallow; and because they have livelier action, many experts prefer them for fishing deep in slow water as well. To carry them deep, some type of weight is attached to the leader.

No one becomes a complete nymph fisherman overnight. Techniques for fishing nymphs are far more numerous and varied than those for any other type of fly. Depending on species and stage of life, the naturals may swim, crawl across the bottom, burrow in it or simply tumble along with the current. So the nymph fisherman can work his fly realistically by drifting it freely with the current, or by twitching or stripping it along at various depths.

Detecting strikes in nymph fishing can be difficult. When you drift a nymph, it may be impossible to feel the take. The best solution is to use some kind of strike indicator (p. 64), such as a piece of yarn or cork, attached to the leader. If you see any twitch or hesitation, set the hook. You can also detect takes simply by watching the tip of your fly line. If you use a sink-tip line, keep an eye on the point where the lighter-colored floating portion disappears below the surface.

Sometimes nymphing fish are visible only as flashes near the streambed as they turn and dart in the current to feed. At other times, their tails make swirls on the surface when they tip nose-down to take nymphs on the bottom, or their backs may break water when they feed on naturals that are only a few inches deep. Anglers often mistake these swirls for rises to adult insects, and make futile attempts to catch the trout with dry flies.

Nymphs usually work best when fished on or near the bottom. To increase the depth of a drift, angle your cast farther upstream so the fly will have more time to sink before reaching the trout. You may have to use a weighted nymph, add weight to your leader or use a sink-tip line to get deep enough.

In the still water of pools, try making a long cast, letting the nymph sink near the bottom, then retrieving it in short twitches. In very cold water, especially in early season, a nymph moved very slowly along the bottom may be more effective than anything else. Stay alert for strikes; a trout may pick up the nymph and drop it instantly.

Streamer Basics

Big trout feed almost exclusively on baitfish, and most streamers are tied on long-shank hooks to mimic the shiners, dace, sculpins, chubs, darters and even young trout so important in the diet of these larger trout. The traditional streamer has a wing of long hackle feathers, but other streamer types have wings made of bucktail, marabou or a strip of rabbit fur.

Not only do streamers attract the attention of big trout better than small flies; they also give you a better chance of hanging on once a fish is hooked. The big, stout hooks hold securely, and the heavy tippets generally used with streamers make break-offs less likely.

Some brightly colored streamers do not closely imitate any baitfish, but instead work as attractor patterns. Often, these bright patterns draw more strikes than realistic ones.

Because of their size and bulk, streamers produce more vibration than other subsurface flies when stripped through the water. This extra attraction helps fish locate them in roily water or after dark. Muddler patterns, with their oversized, clipped deer hair heads, make the most underwater disturbance.

Like nymphs, streamers may be tied weighted or unweighted, and can be fished with floating or sink-tip lines, or with full-sinking lines. Split shot or other weight may be added to the leader as needed.

Streamers can be fished with a variety of retrieves and at almost any depth. Like nymphs, they are extremely effective when fished deep. Use a weighted streamer to search a broad stretch of fast current, or strip an unweighted one across slower water with a steady or erratic retrieve.

Because of their size and wind resistance, streamers are more difficult to cast than most other types of flies. A heavy rod will help you cast a streamer and make it easier to quickly land a big trout.

Wet-Fly Basics

When most anglers think of wet flies, they picture the colorful patterns of a century ago. But the wet flies of today bear little resemblance to these gaudy museum pieces. Although the popularity of wet flies diminished with the introduction of more realistic nymph patterns, there are still good reasons for using wets.

Traditional wet-fly techniques are among the simplest in fly fishing. Generally fished without weight, wet flies are much lighter, smaller and less air-resistant than streamers, so they're easier to cast. And your presentation and retrieve need not be as precise as in fishing with nymphs. Wet flies are commonly used to cover expanses of potential holding water rather than particular lies. But they can be fished to specific targets.

Wet flies have soft, absorbent hackle to help them sink quickly and give them lifelike action. The standard wet has a feather wing; dull-colored patterns of this type are thought to represent drowned adult insects. Feather-wing wets with bright colors and metallic tinsels may suggest tiny baitfish, but serve mainly as attractor patterns, representing nothing in particular.

Today, the most popular wets are *soft-hackle* flies, which are tied without wings and resemble insect larvae, and *palmer-hackle* flies, which have hackle wrapped along their entire length. Commonly called Wooly Worms, these flies are favorites for trout in big western rivers.

Wet flies are a good choice when you are faced with an expanse of unfamiliar water where there are few clues as to where trout may be holding. Casting perpendicular to the bank and allowing the fly to swing across the current lets you search the water more effectively than most other methods of fishing. In slower water, you can strip in a wet fly with a steady or erratic retrieve, as you would a streamer.

Handling Trout

With fishing pressure on most trout streams increasing, catch-and-release fishing is growing in popularity both as a fisheries management tool and as a voluntary measure among conscientious anglers. But catch-and-release fishing does no good unless the fish are handled and released properly.

The faster you land a fish, the better the chance that it will survive. Use the heaviest tippet material practical for the conditions and apply pressure just below the tippet's breaking strength. Allowing a trout to fight for an extended period will exhaust it and may cause a buildup of toxic chemicals in the blood.

Handle the trout as little as possible. The best technique is to grasp the hook with forceps and back it out of the fish's mouth; this way, the trout remains in the water and you do not have to touch it and risk removing its protective slime. A barbless hook (opposite) minimizes handling time. Never squeeze a trout tightly, hold it by the gills, drop it on rocks, beach it or keep it out of water for more than a few seconds.

How to Hold Trout for Photographs

CUP your hand gently under the belly to hold a small- to medium-size trout.

GRASP the tail of a large trout with one hand and support its weight by placing your other hand beneath its belly. Don't hold the fish high above the water; it could slip out of your hand and injure itself.

Tips for Landing and Releasing Trout

MASH down the barb with a forceps or a pair of needlenose pliers. Barbless hooks are required in many fly-fishing waters, because they reduce damage to a fish's mouth.

USE a net made of a soft, fine nylon or cotton mesh and be sure to wet it before netting the fish. This way, you won't remove the trout's protective slime layer or damage its fins. A net also reduces the time needed to land the fish.

RELEASE a trout with its head facing into a moderate current. Strong gill movement indicates the fish is ready to be released. If necessary, rock it back and forth gently to force water over the gills. Never release a fish before it can right itself.

SUBSURFACE
FLY-FISHING
TECHNIQUES

Fishing the Subsurface

It's easy to understand why subsurface techniques are so effective. Trout do the vast majority of their feeding beneath the surface, primarily on or near the bottom. They also do a fair amount of feeding in the mid-depths.

Trout nearly always hold along the bottom unless an abundance of some food form prompts them to feed higher in the water. Here's a simple rule: Always begin by fishing the bottom unless you see signs that they are holding and feeding at some other level.

You may be able to spot trout on the bottom, especially if you wear polarized sunglasses. Look for anything out of the ordinary. Something that moves occasionally in opposition to the current, for instance, might be the finning tail of a big trout. A flash of white could be a trout's mouth opening to inhale drifting insects, or it might be a trout tipping its belly to the side as it takes naturals. A dark shape on a light bottom may be the shadow of a trout hanging invisibly a few inches above it.

Unless you can see them, it may be difficult to determine if trout are feeding in the mid-depths. But there are some good clues. Mayfly duns on the water, for instance, tell you that mayfly nymphs are emerging. If you see duns, but trout are not taking them, chances are they're taking the nymphs.

Trout sometimes feed in the mid-depths on caddisfly pupae swimming up from the bottom. The pupae are easier to catch than the winged adults, which fly away quickly once they reach the surface. When caddisflies are emerging, your clue is the splashy rises trout make as they chase pupae to the surface and break through from momentum.

Most aquatic insects have *drift cycles*. At certain times, usually around dawn or dusk, great numbers of the nymphs or larvae let go of the bottom or weeds and the current carries them downstream. The sudden availability of food often prompts trout to feed heavily in the mid-depths.

On the following pages are the subsurface techniques most effective for fishing the wide variety of water types likely to hold trout.

Shot-and-Indicator Nymphing

This versatile method of presenting nymphs can be used in a wide variety of water types and forms the foundation of many of the subsurface fishing techniques that follow. Used primarily for covering the bottom when trout are scattered over wide areas, this technique can also be effective for targeting fish in specific lies.

The added weight ensures that your fly gets down to the bottom where the fish are most likely to be feeding, while the indicator, a piece of highly visible floating material attached to your leader, lets you monitor what your fly is doing.

The fly should drift naturally, with little drag, so it looks like a dislodged nymph drifting freely in the current. If you see drag on your indicator, chances are the nymph is not drifting freely. Depending on the current pattern between you and the indicator, you must throw upstream or downstream mends to eliminate drag. To further ensure a drag-free drift, be sure there is some slack line between your rod tip and the indicator.

As the weight ticks along the gravel and stones on the bottom, the indicator may twitch slightly on the surface. Any sudden jerk or pause in the indicator, however, may signal that a trout has taken the fly. Learning to read the indicator is the key to becoming a better nymph fisherman. Once you become more proficient at detecting strikes, you may not need the indicator.

Ideal waters for shot-and-indicator nymphing are featureless runs from 2 to 4 feet deep with a moderate current. Here, trout may hold anywhere on the bottom and the angler must present a nymph systematically throughout the run. The technique is less suitable for slower water where the disturbance of the shot entering the water is more likely to spook wary fish. It is also less effective in heavy, fast water, where it may be difficult to get the fly to the bottom. There, the Brooks method (p. 96) would be a better choice.

the Brooks method (p. 96) would be a better choice.

THE STRIKE INDICATOR DEBATE

Some old-time fly fishermen frown on the use of strike indicators, likening them to bobbers used for live bait fishing. But renowned fly angler Lefty Kreh doesn't see it that way.

"They resent the fact that newcomers to the sport did not spend their time on the water learning to do it the hard way — as they did.

"Whether or not you use an indicator is a personal thing. If you don't like them, don't use them. But if they work for you and you enjoy using them, I urge you to continue."

Lefty Kreh

ADVANCED FLY FISHING TECHNIQUES

Equipment for Shot-and-Indicator Nymphing

The heavy shot and wind-resistant indicator make casting this rig more difficult than casting a simple leader-and-fly setup. The leader tends to hinge at the split shot and tangle easily, particularly when cast with a fast-action rod. A medium-action rod helps open your loops to prevent these tangles.

Use a long fly rod, 8½ to 9½ feet, for easier line mending. A weight-forward line is recommended for turning over the heavily weighted leader. It also helps load the rod more easily on the short casts typical of this nymphing method.

You'll need a leader that's long enough for attaching an indicator while still allowing the fly to get to the bottom. In typical shot-and-indicator water, an 8-foot leader is sufficient. For water deeper than 4 feet or in slightly faster current, choose a longer leader, up to 12 feet.

The two-fly rig (opposite) gives you better coverage and helps you discover the best fly more quickly. Try nymphs of different types or ones that differ greatly in size or color.

TYPES OF WEIGHTS

POPULAR WEIGHTS include: (1) lead or lead-substitute split shot, (2) twist-on lead strips and (3) moldable tungsten compound.

TYPES OF INDICATORS

INDICATORS include (1) corkie, (2) synthetic yarn, (3) float putty and (4) twist-on.

FLIES FOR SHOT-AND-INDICATOR NYMPHING

POPULAR FLIES include: (1) Gold Ribbed Hare's Ear, (2) Muskrat, (3) Fox Squirrel and (4) Herl Nymph.

HOW TO MAKE A SHOT-AND-INDICATOR RIG

ADD *an 8- to 10-inch tippet section. Anything longer allows the fly to drift out of the feeding zone at the bottom.*

POSITION *the indicator up the leader approximately twice the depth of the water in most situations. In slower current, place the indicator up the leader only slightly more than the water depth; in faster current, about 3 times the water depth.*

ATTACH *the weight to the leader just above the tippet knot. Use only enough weight to get your fly to the bottom. When using split shot, attach several small ones instead of one large one. This way, you can easily make fine adjustments.*

HOW TO MAKE A TWO-FLY RIG

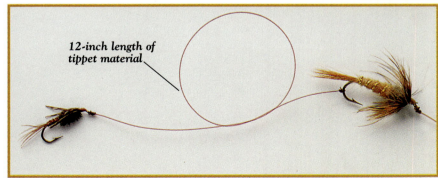

12-inch length of tippet material

TIE *a dropper fly (left) to a 12-inch length of tippet material that is lighter than the leader tippet. Attach the other end of the material to the hook bend of the main fly (right), using an improved clinch knot (p. 73).*

Casting Shot-and-Indicator Rigs

Conventional fly casting calls for tight loops, false casting and high line speed for distance and pinpoint accuracy. But a shot-and-indicator rig requires a different casting style. Because of the added weight and indicator, the line is more difficult to control and tangles more easily. And if a split shot or weighted nymph strikes your graphite fly rod, it could easily shatter.

By using shorter casts, from 20 to 45 feet, and open-loop casting (below), you can keep the fly, weight and indicator separated to better

HOW TO MAKE AN OPEN-LOOP CAST

1 STOP the rod crisply on the backcast, then lower the rod tip slightly to open the loop and give the leader and shot plenty of room to pass the fly line. Allow the line to straighten completely before beginning the forward cast.

2 STOP the rod crisply on the forward cast, then lower the rod tip again to open the loop. If you held your rod in the normal position at the end of the forward cast, the loop would be much tighter (dashed line), increasing the chance of the line tangling or the weight striking the rod.

control the weight and keep it from tangling. Keeping false casting to a minimum also reduces the problem. One way to eliminate false casting is to let the current load your rod at the end of a drift so you can make a lob cast (below).

One of the difficulties many beginning anglers experience in trying to cast a shot-and-indicator rig is that the extra weight causes the line to hit the water when attempting to false cast. To prevent this problem, aim your cast higher than normal.

The two casting methods shown on these pages will make it easier to cast a shot-and-indicator rig.

HOW TO MAKE A LOB CAST (WATER LOADING)

1 LET the current take out line until all slack is removed and the current lifts the fly and shot to the surface. Pivot to face upstream.

2 MAKE a forward cast, lobbing the fly upstream. If you're having trouble lifting the heavy rig off the water, make a short tug on the line with your line hand as you make the cast.

1 QUARTER your cast upstream of the water you want to fish. The shorter the cast, the more control you'll have over the drift of the fly. Your line should land on the water pointing straight toward the indicator.

Current

2 FOLLOW the drift of the indicator with your rod tip. Mend the line as necessary to keep the indicator and fly drifting naturally. As the indicator drifts toward you, draw in slack with your line hand and raise your rod to lift line off the water (shown). This way, conflicting currents won't cause drag.

3 PIVOT downstream as the indicator passes your position. To prolong the drift, lower your rod (shown) and feed line through the guides. Wait a few seconds at the end of the drift to let the current pull the slack out of the line. Then, make an upstream lob cast, covering the water as shown on the opposite page.

ESTABLISH *a casting grid that suits the water you're fishing. In this situation, quarter your first cast upstream, to point A, and allow the rig to drift straight downstream. Make additional casts and drifts at 2- to 5-foot intervals, to points B, C and D. Then, move upstream a few steps and repeat the procedure.*

Hinged-Leader Nymphing

One of the toughest things in nymph fishing is knowing exactly where your fly is in relation to your indicator. Unseen currents can pull a nymph in many directions during a single drift, making strike detection difficult. Hinged-leader nymphing, an alternative to the standard shot-and-indicator method, helps overcome the problem.

The technique, best described by veteran fly-fishing guide, John Judy, involves building a leader that forms a right angle and suspends the nymph directly below the strike indicator. This way, the fly and indicator drift in the same column of water, reducing the effect of conflicting currents, which, in turn, reduces drag. Because you need less weight than in standard shot-and-indicator nymphing, the fly has a more natural action. And with the fly directly below the indicator, rather than angling away from it, takes are much easier to detect.

Like shot-and-indicator nymphing, the hinged-leader technique is most effective for covering broad runs with even flow and a fairly uniform depth of 2 to 5 feet. It does not work as well in water of varying depths. When your line reaches a deep hole, the indicator keeps the nymph from reaching bottom. The technique is ideal when fish are feeding in the mid-depths, because the fly stays at a consistent depth.

Because of the long, right-angle tippet, this rig may be more difficult to cast than some other nymphing rigs. The techniques shown on pages 66 to 67 will solve most of your casting problems.

A HINGED LEADER keeps the fly drifting directly below the indicator, in the same current lane. With a standard shot-and-indicator rig (inset), the fly may drift in a different current lane.

Equipment for the Hinged-Leader Technique

You can tailor a hinged leader to your fishing by adjusting the size of the indicator, weight of the fly and length of the tippet.

The indicator is made from a section of highly buoyant polypropylene yarn, such as Maxi-cord®. High-vis colors, such as bright yellow or pink, are recommended. Carry a small pair

HOW TO MAKE A HINGED LEADER

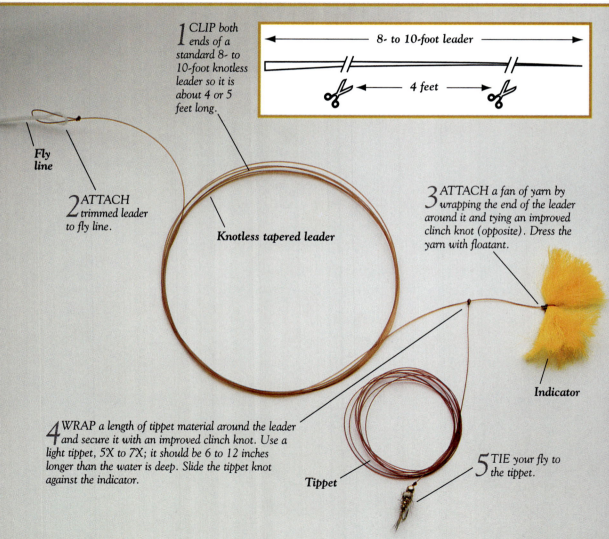

1 CLIP both ends of a standard 8- to 10-foot knotless leader so it is about 4 or 5 feet long.

8- to 10-foot leader

4 feet

Fly line

2 ATTACH trimmed leader to fly line.

Knotless tapered leader

3 ATTACH a fan of yarn by wrapping the end of the leader around it and tying an improved clinch knot (opposite). Dress the yarn with floatant.

Indicator

4 WRAP a length of tippet material around the leader and secure it with an improved clinch knot. Use a light tippet, 5X to 7X; it should be 6 to 12 inches longer than the water is deep. Slide the tippet knot against the indicator.

Tippet

5 TIE your fly to the tippet.

of scissors to trim the indicator to the desired size, which depends on the weight of the fly and the turbulence of the water. Dress the indicator with floatant to keep it floating high.

Any type of nymph will work as long as it is weighted just enough to keep it drifting at a right angle to the indicator. A split shot is not normally used, but you can add one if necessary.

Use an 8½- to 9½-foot, 6- to 8-weight rod to cast the weighted fly and wind-resistant indicator and for easy line mending. A double-taper line helps you make the initial roll-cast mend, shown on page 74.

HOW TO ATTACH TIPPET TO LEADER WITH IMPROVED CLINCH KNOT

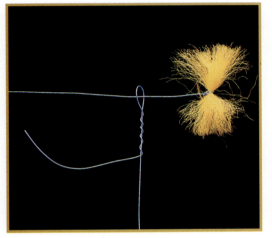

1 WRAP *tippet around leader, and wind tag end around standing end 5 times.*

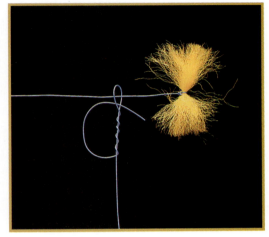

2 PASS *tag end through opening closest to leader.*

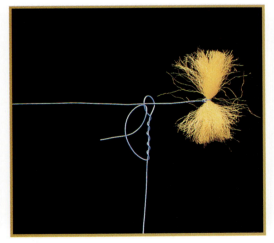

3 BRING *tag end back through loop, as shown.*

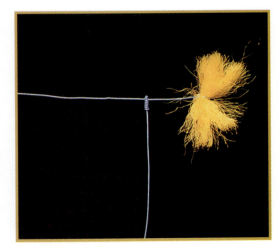

4 SNUG *up knot by first moistening the wraps and then pulling on tag and standing ends. Trim tag.*

1 QUARTER your cast upstream and across current. Keep your first cast short and gradually lengthen subsequent casts, as you would in the shot-and-indicator technique (p. 69).

Current

2 MAKE a roll cast straight at the indicator. Called a roll-cast mend, *this line-control method repositions the indicator upstream of the fly.* This way, the indicator does not cause drag on the fly, so it sinks straight down and drifts directly below the indicator. The mend should be just strong enough to lift the indicator off the water without lifting the nymph. The indicator will drift a little faster than the nymph; when it gets ahead far enough to cause drag, make another roll-cast mend.

3 LIFT *the rod and strip in line as the indicator drifts toward you. This takes up slack between the rod tip and indicator. Maintain about the amount of slack shown; if you strip in line too fast and remove all the slack, the line will cause drag on the fly.*

4 PAY OUT *line as the indicator drifts past you to extend your drift. Set the hook at any hesitation or turn of the indicator. Make casts of increasing length until the section of water has been covered.*

The weighted nymph technique works best in clear spring creeks.

Weighted Nymph Technique

On slow spring creeks and smooth, clear runs of larger freestone streams, you'll often see trout holding and feeding on the bottom in water 2 to 3 feet deep. Drop a standard shot-and-indicator rig into the water, however, and you'll instantly spook the trout. A weighted nymph fished on a long leader is better suited for sight fishing trout on the bottom.

The long leader, 12 to 14 feet, keeps the fly line as far from the trout as possible, reducing the chances of alarming fish in the clear water. The tippet should be very light, 5X to 7X, for minimum visibility. On this rig, weighted nymphs in sizes 12 to 20 sink quickly and easily reach bottom with no added weight. To cast the long, light leader, use a 3- to 5-weight rod from 8 to 9 feet long.

When you see a trout feeding on the bottom, try to present the nymph within inches of its nose and watch for the white flash as its mouth opens to take the fly. If you're having trouble noticing takes, try attaching a small yarn strike indicator in a natural color. It will land softly, and the color won't attract the fish's attention.

The weighted nymph technique is not a good choice for fishing blind, because the extra-long leader makes it difficult to detect a take.

FLIES FOR THE WEIGHTED NYMPH TECHNIQUE

*POPULAR FLIES
include: (1) Bead-
head Pheasant Tail,
(2) Bead-head Hare's
Ear, (3) Brassie,
(4) Olive Scud,
(5) Prince Nymph
and (6) Blue-wing
Olive Nymph.*

HOW TO FISH A WEIGHTED NYMPH

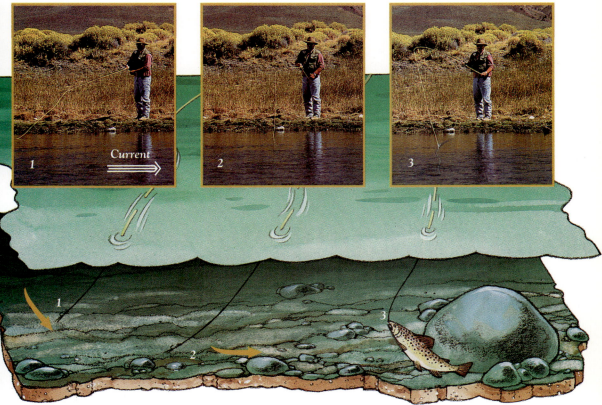

1 CAST *upstream of a visible trout's lie from 5 to 15 feet, depending on water depth and current speed, to give the fly time to sink. False cast to measure distance, but do so sidearm and not directly over the trout.*

2 FOLLOW *the drift with your rod tip as the fly sinks to the bottom. Take up excess slack with your line hand, but don't draw the line so tight that it causes drag on the fly. Mend as little as possible; too much mending will spook the fish.*

3 WATCH *the trout closely. If you see a take, set the hook gently to prevent breaking the light leader and to avoid alarming the fish should you fail to hook it. If the fly is too far from the trout, complete the drift so you won't spook it, and cast again. It may take several drifts before the fly arrives at the right depth at the right moment.*

ON SPOTTING TROUT

Upstream nymphing to visible trout in spring creeks and slow, clear pools requires sharp eyesight.... You may see the trout move to take a nymph; you might spot his shadow, or see him as an indistinct shape on the bottom. Seldom will you get a good look at the fish, and often you'll fish to a stick or light-colored rock before you realize it's not a trout.

Tom Rosenbauer

THE ORVIS FLY-FISHING GUIDE

Upstream Dead Drift

A nymph or wet fly cast directly upstream and allowed to drift over a trout's lie can be very effective for imitating free-drifting food forms. The upstream dead drift also helps avoid the drag that results from casting across conflicting currents, because the fly line, leader and fly all drift in a straight line.

The technique is most effective in slow to moderate current from 1 to 3 feet deep. In most cases, you're casting to a visible trout or a probable lie, and this technique enables you to approach from directly downstream, so the fish won't see you. In narrow streams with heavily vegetated banks, this may be the only way of presenting a fly to the fish.

FLIES FOR THE UPSTREAM DEAD-DRIFT TECHNIQUE

POPULAR FLIES include: nymphs, such as (1) Red Squirrel, (2) Prince, (3) Zug Bug; and wet flies, such as (4) Partridge and Green, (5) Alder, and (6) Partridge and Yellow.

You can use the upstream dead drift to fish at most any level. To reach trout holding on the bottom, tie on a weighted nymph and cast well upstream of the lie so the fly has sufficient time to sink; add split shot if necessary. For trout in the mid-depths, use an unweighted nymph or wet fly, and don't cast upstream as far.

Casting upstream has its drawbacks, however. In clear, smooth water, the leader and line will fall directly over the trout, likely spooking it. To prevent this problem, use a reach cast (p. 80) to place the leader and line slightly off to one side. It also helps to use a long leader, 9 to 12 feet, with a 4X to 6X tippet. Even if the leader floats right over trout, they probably won't notice it.

Select a 4- to 6-weight rod from 7½ to 9 feet long. Rods at the shorter end of this range are best in narrow, brushy streams. Those at the longer end work better for making reach casts. Some anglers use a yarn indicator, which lands more gently than other types.

1 STAND directly downstream from your target and cast upstream. When fishing smooth water, false cast off to one side and use a reach cast (shown) to keep the line from spooking the fish. If the surface of the water is broken, you can cast straight upstream without disturbing the trout. Cast far enough above the lie to allow the fly to sink to the fish's level.

Current

2 TAKE up line as the fly drifts toward you to remove excess slack and allow you to set the hook quickly. Do not draw the line or leader tight, however, or the fly will not drift naturally. If you see the line twitch or feel a take, or if the fish suddenly moves toward the fly, gently set the hook.

3 LIFT your rod at the end of the drift so you can make a roll-cast pickup (opposite). This is the easiest way to pick up line when it is rapidly drifting toward you, and it minimizes disturbance on the water, so you won't spook the fish. When you have made several drifts in one location, move upstream or sideways to the next lie and repeat the presentation.

HOW TO MAKE A ROLL-CAST PICKUP

1 RAISE your rod slowly as the fly passes the lie and the line is still on the water in front of you. Stop the rod when it is slightly behind you (shown). Accelerate steadily, then make a short speed stroke.

2 STOP the rod quickly while the rod tip is moving in the direction you want the line to go. Let the fly line roll out in front of you; it should form an elliptical loop and straighten out above the water.

3 MAKE a normal backcast and then a normal forward cast or reach cast, and let the line, leader and fly settle to the water.

You need slow, clear water for the Sawyer method.

The Sawyer Method

Catching trout in the clear, slow water of a fertile spring creek can be a challenge to even the most experienced fly fisherman. Because they're so vulnerable to predators, trout are super-wary, and the abundant food supply means they rarely have to move very far for a meal. The late Frank Sawyer, riverkeeper on the Wiltshire Avon in England for over fifty years, pioneered the technique of sight fishing to trout in clear water with uniform currents. He discovered that by drifting a nymph directly to a visible fish feeding over a weedbed or otherwise holding in the mid-depths, he could induce a take.

The key to the Sawyer method is learning to read the speed of the current and knowing how quickly your nymph sinks. Then you'll know how far to cast upstream so the current will deliver your nymph precisely to the trout.

At first glance, this technique seems very simple, but it requires a great deal of practice to place the fly within inches of the trout, with no drag. The take may not be obvious; the fish just opens its mouth and sips in the fly, so you'll have to watch intently. Pay attention to the fish, but also watch the point where the leader enters the water. If the leader shows any unusual movement, gently set the hook.

This delicate method requires light equipment. Use a 7½- to 9-foot, 2- to 5-weight rod, a floating line and a 9- to 12-foot leader with a 5X to 7X tippet. You don't need a precise nymph imitation. A wide variety of impressionistic searching patterns, usually unweighted, can be used.

The Sawyer method is not a good choice in streams where the water is too turbulent to spot trout. Nor is it effective for visible trout on the bottom, because the fly will not sink deep enough.

HOW TO USE THE SAWYER METHOD

Current

1 POSITION your-self downstream and across current from a visible trout. Keep a low profile, using the streamside vegetation as camouflage. Cast far enough upstream of the fish so the nymph has time to sink to the fish's feeding level. Whenever possible, use a sidearm cast to keep your rod tip out of the trout's window of vision.

2 FOLLOW the drift of the fly with your rod tip. Watch the fish for any sign of a take, such as the white of its mouth or a sudden movement. You may have to drift the fly to the fish several times to entice a take. Set the hook gently so you won't snap the fine tippet.

FLIES FOR THE SAWYER METHOD

1
2
3
4

POPULAR FLIES include: (1) Pheasant tail Nymph, developed by Sawyer to imitate a swimming nymph; (2) Quill Gordon Nymph; (3) Orange Scud and (4) Black Quill Nymph.

The Leisenring Lift

WHY THE LEISENRING LIFT?

The hackles or legs start to work, opening and closing, and our trout is backing downstream in order to watch the fly a little more, because he is not quite persuaded yet. Now you can see the fly become even more deadly. As more water flows against the line, the fly rises higher off the bottom and the hackle is working in every fiber. It will jump out of the water in a minute, now, and the trout is coming for it. Bang! He's got it.

James Leisenring

THE ART OF TYING THE WET FLY

Few nymphing techniques have proven as enduring as the Leisenring lift; and, when done correctly, few are as deadly at taking trout. First described by James Leisenring and V. S. Hidy in *The Art of Tying the Wet Fly* (Crown, 1941), this technique gives any nymph or wet-fly pattern a lifelike action and is effective for imitating aquatic insects rising toward the surface to emerge. Yet it will frequently trigger a strike even at times when no hatch is underway.

Leisenring recognized that trout eagerly chase these rising insects, their momentum sometimes making them break the surface. He found that he could imitate the rising arc of the natural by drifting a nymph to within a foot or two of the trout and then stopping the rod, which caused the current to lift the fly, as if it were swimming to the surface to emerge.

This method is equally effective for sight fishing in slow, clear spring creeks and targeting obvious lies in freestone rivers with broad, even currents of moderate speed. As in the Sawyer method (p. 82), you must know the current speed and sink rate of your nymph so you can present it at precisely the level of a visible trout. When fishing to lies, plan your drift so the fly is on the bottom as it approaches the lie, and then stop it so it rises just ahead of the lie.

Although Leisenring merely stopped the rod so the current lifted the fly, many modern-day practitioners have modified the technique by not only stopping the rod, but raising it at the same time. This way, the fly rises faster, for what some believe is an even more enticing action.

The equipment and flies used for the Leisenring lift are very similar to those used for the Sawyer method. But because trout commonly feed on rising caddis pupae, caddis imitations are also effective.

How To Make the Leisenring Lift

Current

1 STAND *across current and slightly upstream of a visible trout or known lie. Cast far enough upstream of your target to allow the nymph to sink to the fish's feeding level 2 to 4 feet before reaching the lie.*

2 FOLLOW *the drift of the fly with your rod, keeping the tip low. Mend the line as necessary to keep the fly drifting naturally (shown).*

3 STOP the rod so the fly drifts to within about a foot
of the trout or a known lie. The pressure of the current on the leader will begin to lift the fly. If you're fishing to a lie rather than a visible trout, vary the point at
which you stop the rod on subsequent drifts, so you
cover the entire lie.

4 LIFT the rod, if desired, to make the fly rise more
quickly. When you detect a take, set the hook gently.

The Wet-Fly Swing

UNIFORM COVERAGE

The wet fly fisherman will cover the water best if he extends his casting range by a uniform distance each time. If, as he starts casting, he lengthens his cast by about a yard each time until he reaches the casting distance he wishes to maintain down through the run, and then takes a single step between each cast, he will have his fly pass within eighteen inches, vertically, of every fish within his casting range. Uniform coverage leaves no blank spots where the biggest fish in the pool might escape having the fly come within striking range.

Lee Wulff

TROUT ON
A FLY

The wet-fly swing is one of the oldest techniques for presenting a subsurface fly to trout and is a longtime favorite among Atlantic salmon fishermen. Unlike other techniques, where drag is carefully avoided, the wet-fly swing actually employs drag to give the fly action and quickly cover the water. The force of the water on the line causes the fly to dart across the current, mimicking the action of a variety of food forms, including baitfish, immature aquatic insects and even terrestrials. With the fly passing crosswise in the current, the fish gets a good look at the side of the fly.

By controlling the amount of belly in the line, the fisherman can regulate the speed and angle of the fly as it swings across the current. The more belly, the faster the current will drag the fly. The pressure on the line also helps set the hook when a trout takes the fly.

The wet-fly swing works well in all types of water and current speeds, but is most effective at depths of 5 feet or less. Ideal for searching large sections of river, the technique works equally well for trout, steelhead or salmon, and can be used with large or small wet flies, streamers and even nymphs.

The technique is normally used to cover water with numerous lies, such as a long run with many boulders on the bottom, but it also enables you to sweep the fly past a specific lie, such as a log that is perpendicular to the current.

No special equipment is required for the wet-fly swing, but many anglers prefer a long rod, from 8½ to 9½ feet, so they can mend and control the fly line more easily. A floating line with an 8- to 10-foot leader works well in most situations. Many anglers use a two-fly rig (p. 65) for additional coverage.

Current

1 MAKE *a short cast across the current to work lies that are out and downstream from you. The angle of your cast depends on the speed of the current. In swift water, cast slightly downstream to minimize the belly and keep the line from being pulled downstream too quickly. In slower current, cast slightly upstream so more belly will form and speed up the fly.*

2 MEND *your line to control the speed of your fly. If the fly swings too slowly, make a downstream mend (shown) to increase belly and accelerate the fly. If your fly is swinging too quickly, throw an upstream mend to reduce the belly and slow the fly.*

3 LET *the fly swing until it hangs in the current below you and begins to rise. You'll get a high percentage of your strikes at this point.*

4 LENGTHEN *each subsequent cast by 1 to 3 feet until you've thoroughly covered all the water you can reach from your position. Then, take a step or two downstream and repeat the process.*

High-Sticking in Pocket Water

Among the most productive types of trout water are boulder-strewn, medium- to high-gradient streams with plenty of pocket water. The eddies that form upstream and downstream of the boulders and the plunge pools and scour holes that form around them hold surprising numbers of good-size trout that rarely see a fly.

But pocket water can be very difficult to fish, explaining why it sees so little fishing pressure. Casting a line to a small eddy across these wild, conflicting currents means almost instant drag. Even if you do get your fly into one of these pockets, it's almost impossible to get it down to the bottom.

High-sticking can help you reach trout in pocket water. The technique involves making a series of controlled, short-line drifts, lifting your rod high above the water to take up slack as it forms. This keeps as much line as possible off the water so the current will not whisk the fly out of the pocket as soon as it lands. And with the current catching only the leader, rather than the whole line, the fly sinks more quickly. High-sticking originated centuries ago as a method of dapping dry flies into pocket water, but today's anglers have found that it works equally well with subsurface flies.

Trout seldom move far to feed in the swift water, so you must present the fly within inches of their lie. You may have to make as many as 10 drifts through a given pocket to cover it thoroughly. By taking up slack with the rod rather than your line hand, you maintain better contact with the fly throughout the drift for easier strike detection and quicker hook sets.

Although you must get close to the fish with this technique, the turbulent water breaks up your silhouette. High-sticking will not work in slow, smooth water where the fish can easily see you approaching.

FLIES FOR HIGH-STICKING

POPULAR NYMPHS for high-sticking include: (1) Bead-head Pheasant Tail, (2) Bead-head Hare's Ear, (3) Montana Stone and (4) Bitch Creek.

1 APPROACH the pocket from downstream and slightly off to the side, so the debris you kick up doesn't drift over the fish. Get as close as you can, preferably within 10 to 15 feet. Any farther and you'll have difficulty lifting enough line off the water. Make a short lob cast (shown), dropping the fly onto the water 2 to 5 feet upstream of the suspected lie.

An 8½- to 9½- foot rod is recommended for high-sticking. A long rod makes it easier to lift the line off the water to control slack. Since little casting is required, most any type of floating line will do. Use a leader from 7½ to 9 feet long so you can keep most or all of the fly line out of the water. The more turbulent the water, the heavier your leader can be. Use a 3X to 5X tippet in most situations.

A wide variety of subsurface flies, preferably searching patterns that represent a broad range of insect life, will work for this technique. Trout holding along the edge of fast current have little time to inspect your offering; they just dart into the current and grab it. In heavy water, choose a bead-head nymph or other weighted fly.

A strike indicator is seldom needed; because you are using such a short line, you are always in close contact with the fly, making it easy to detect a take. Most anglers just concentrate on the tip of their fly line. If you do use an indicator, however, it should be a high-visibility, high-floating type that shows up well in rough water. Attach it up your leader approximately twice the water depth.

HOW TO HIGH-STICK POCKET WATER

Current

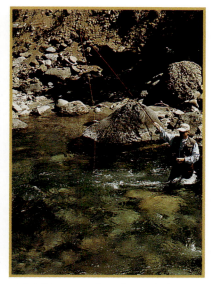

2 RAISE your rod to take up slack as the fly drifts toward you. Lift as much line off the water as you can, but do not strip in line.

3 LOWER the rod as the fly passes your position to lengthen the drift. Let the current straighten your line at the end of the drift; then make another lob cast and repeat.

How To Cover Water with the High-Sticking Method

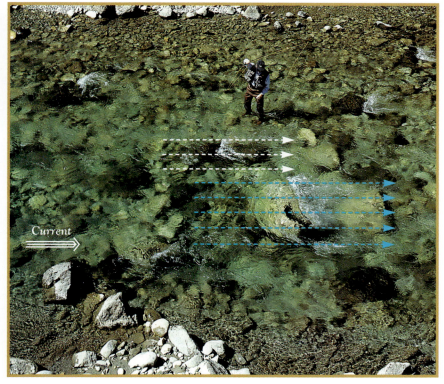

Current

MAKE a series of casts to a boulder. Begin by working the side of the boulder nearest you, reaching out slightly farther on each subsequent drift, until you thoroughly cover the upstream and downstream pockets (white arrows). After working a boulder thoroughly, move upstream or out and work another boulder (blue arrows).

The Brooks Method

DEMANDING BUT EFFECTIVE

The tackle one must use to fish the deep runs does not appeal to some – the light-tackle people especially. Such fishing requires a rod of eight or nine feet to control the drift, and with enough backbone to raise thirty feet of deeply sunken line and a weighted nymph and hurl it back upstream without false casting. False casting a heavy weighted nymph is a form of Russian roulette with eyes and ears as stakes.

Charles Brooks

NYMPH FISHING FOR LARGER TROUT

Originated by the late fly-fishing legend, Charles Brooks, this technique is ideal for delivering big, weighted nymphs to large trout in deep, swift water. Brooks, who lived just outside the town of West Yellowstone, Montana, developed his method on the famous rivers of that region, including the Madison, Gallatin and Yellowstone, and the Box Canyon stretch of the Henry's Fork. Brooks found that the largest trout hug the bottom in deep, boulder-filled runs where the current speed approaches 8 miles per hour. These big fish rarely move for a dry fly, and nymphs on light tackle do not get down deep enough to be effective.

The Brooks method is similar to high-sticking (p. 93) in its short-line approach and in the way line slack is controlled by raising the rod rather than retrieving it during the drift. But the differences are significant: short leaders, sometimes with added weight; sinking lines; and heavily weighted nymphs are needed in the faster, deeper water.

Brooks even designed a number of fly patterns (p. 98) specifically tailored to heavy, turbulent currents.

An 8- to 9-foot rod, preferably an 8- or 9-weight, is recommended to handle the weighted line, leader and fly and to horse big trout out of heavy current. Brooks used a 4- to 6-foot leader to keep the strong current from lifting the fly off the bottom, but you can go as short as 3 feet. A Duncan loop (p. 99) allows the fly to move freely on the stiff leader.

Despite the technique's effectiveness, some anglers shy away from the Brooks method because of the heavy tackle and physical casting style it requires. And the fast, boulder-strewn rivers can challenge even the most experienced waders. But if you're after big trout in big water, the Brooks method is unsurpassed for getting your nymph to the bottom.

HOW TO RIG FOR THE BROOKS METHOD

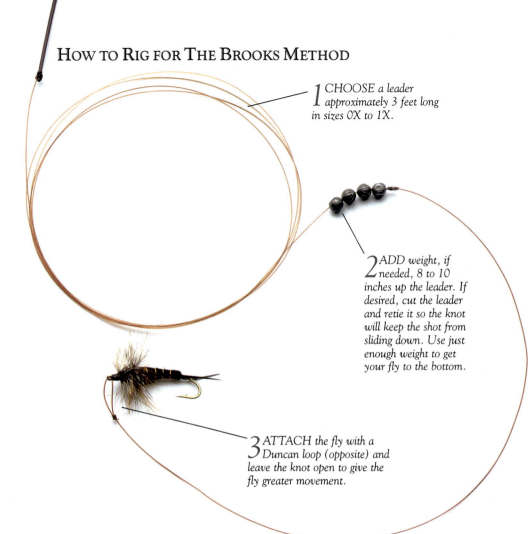

1 CHOOSE *a leader approximately 3 feet long in sizes 0X to 1X.*

2 ADD *weight, if needed, 8 to 10 inches up the leader. If desired, cut the leader and retie it so the knot will keep the shot from sliding down. Use just enough weight to get your fly to the bottom.*

3 ATTACH *the fly with a Duncan loop (opposite) and leave the knot open to give the fly greater movement.*

FLIES FOR THE BROOKS METHOD

POPULAR FLIES *include: (1) Brooks Stone and (2) Skunk Hair Caddis, both designed by Charles Brooks. Other effective flies include: (3) Woolly Bugger and (4) Hellgrammite. The large flies, generally sizes 2 to 6, appeal to large trout, which usually ignore small food items because they're not worth the energy expended to get them. And large flies are easily seen in the turbulent water.*

How to Attach a Fly Using a Duncan Loop

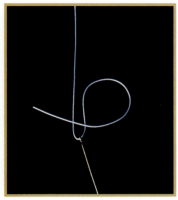

1 PASS tag end through hook eye. Form loop in tag end, as shown.

(plain hook used for clarity)

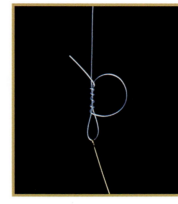

2 PASS tag end through loop. Wind tag end through loop and around standing line 4 times, winding away from hook.

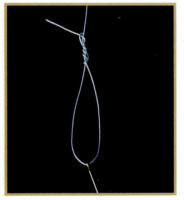

3 MOISTEN wraps and pull tag end to snug up knot.

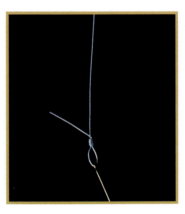

4 SLIDE knot to desired position by pulling on standing line. Trim tag.

Tips for Brooks-Style Fishing

CARRY *a wading staff to help keep your balance in fast water with a bottom of slippery boulders.*

WADING BOOTS *with felt soles and metal studs give you maximum traction.*

1 LOOK for places where the fast water drops into deeper, boulder-filled channels. Stand 4 to 6 feet to the side and slightly upstream from the water you plan to fish. Cast upstream about 15 feet and about 6 feet out (shown).

2 AIM the rod tip above the point where the leader enters the water as the fly moves downstream. This allows the fly to sink; it should be on the bottom as it reaches a point 6 feet out from where you are standing.

3 LIFT the rod tip to take up and control any slack in the line, as you would when high-sticking (p. 95). The longer the cast, the higher you'll need to lift the rod. Do not take in line with your line hand during the drift.

4 PIVOT slightly to follow your fly. As the line swings directly downstream from you, lower your rod tip to extend the drift. Wait several seconds after the line swings downstream. This eliminates all underwater slack, loads the rod and allows you to recast upstream, using a lob cast (p. 67).

The Deep Streamer Swing

When faced with a section of big, deep water, such as a wide pool or broad run, many anglers fail to cover every possible lie, bypassing numbers of trout. The deep streamer swing is the best method for sweeping a fly across the bottom of a broad reach of water to cover it thoroughly and work unseen lies. The technique is also valuable for fishing big, deep rivers, where you can wade safely only at the edges.

The deep streamer swing is similar to the wet-fly swing (p. 88) in that you're casting across-stream and letting the current swing the fly

FLIES FOR THE DEEP STREAMER SWING

POPULAR FLIES include: (1) Woolly Bugger, (2) Spuddler, (3) Gray Ghost and (4) Hare Sculpin.

in concentric arcs through an area with many potential lies. The main differences are that you're fishing bigger water with heavier tackle and larger flies. And the flies are fished on the bottom, rather than in the mid-depths.

Large streamer patterns that imitate minnows, sculpins and leeches are commonly used, but the technique works equally well with big weighted nymphs, such as stonefly and hellgrammite imitations.

Most anglers use 7- to 9-weight sink-tip lines for handling the large flies and getting them to the bottom in the strong current. Depending on the depth and current speed, use a slow to ultrafast sinking tip section from 5 to 24 feet long. In very swift water, you may need a full-sinking line; in a wide river, a shooting-head line. The leader should be short, from 3 to 6 feet, with a 0X to 3X tippet. A very long fly rod, 9 to 10 feet, is the best choice for making long casts with the heavy-sinking or shooting-head lines. This type of rod also makes line mending much easier.

How to Use the Deep Streamer Swing

1 CAST perpendicular to the current and slightly upstream of the water you want to fish. How far upstream depends on water depth and current speed.

Current

2 LET the current take the line downstream, following it with your rod tip. In slow current, you may have to make downstream mends to accelerate the fly; in fast water, upstream mends to slow it.

3 RAISE and lower the rod tip throughout the drift, if desired, to give the fly an erratic darting motion that will often trigger strikes.

MAKE *a short cast from position 1 so the fly lands just upstream from the area you want to fish. Allow the fly to swing along arc A. Lengthen each subsequent cast by 1 to 3 feet, so the fly cover arcs B, C and D. When you've thoroughly covered the water from position 1, take a step or two downstream and repeat the process from position 2. Continue moving downstream until the entire area has been covered.*

The Countdown Method

First described by Ray Bergman in his classic book, *Trout* (Knopf, 1938), the countdown method is primarily a searching technique for helping you identify the level at which the fish are feeding. It is most effective in slow-moving pools, backwaters and large eddies, where trout may hold anywhere from the bottom to several feet above it. This water attracts schools of baitfish and, as a result, large trout.

As the name of the technique suggests, you simply cast out your fly, count while it sinks and then retrieve it slowly to keep it at the same level as long as possible. Use a hand-twist retrieve to mimic the action of a natural aquatic insect, or a slightly erratic strip retrieve for imitating baitfish or crayfish. If you feel a take, repeat the same count on the next cast. If you don't, keep adding a few seconds to the count until a fish hits. The countdown method is not well suited to fast water; your fly would be quickly swept away, giving you much less depth control.

Bergman's original technique involved "blind striking," or setting the hook on a certain count, whether or not he actually felt a hit. Today, with more sensitive equipment, most anglers wait to feel a take before setting the hook.

Most any subsurface fly, including streamers, nymphs and wets, can be used with this technique. The type of line depends mainly on the water depth. In water no deeper than 5 feet, you can get by with a floating line. In deeper water, you'll need a sink-tip or full-sinking line, and possibly a weighted fly or a split shot, to stay down. With a floating line, use a 9- to 12-foot leader and a 3X to 5X tippet; with a sinking line, a 3- to 6-foot leader and a 0X to 3X tippet.

A 6- to 8-weight rod from 8½ to 10 feet long is the best choice for the coundown method, because it enables you to make long casts with a sinking line.

ORIGIN OF COUNTDOWN METHOD

Because we noted that all hits came just at the moment we were likely to get snagged, we decided to see just how long it took for the fly to reach bottom. To ascertain this, we counted. Before long we knew exactly how much to count for the fly to reach a point just above the snags, and when we got that we started striking at the very moment the total count was reached. About every fifth cast, our blind strike was rewarded with a trout.

Ray Bergman
TROUT

FLIES FOR THE COUNTDOWN METHOD

HOW TO COVER WATER WITH THE COUNTDOWN METHOD

POPULAR FLIES include: (1) Clouser Minnow, (2) Black Matuka, (3) Grizzly King, (4) Black Marabou Muddler, (5) Clouser's Crayfish, (6) Bead-head Hare's Ear, (7) Yellow Wooly Worm.

1 POSITION yourself along the edge of a slow pool or eddy, and cast toward deep water.

2 COUNT steadily as the fly sinks. When it reaches level A, about 2 feet down, begin a slow retrieve. Be sure to work the shallower fish first; if you start deep, you may spook the fish that are holding shallower.

3 ADD several seconds to the count on subsequent casts, enough to sink the fly 1 to 2 feet deeper on each. Let's say you hook a fish at level C. You then fan-cast all the deep water you can reach from that position, repeating the same count.

4 KEEP increasing your count after thoroughly working level C. In the example, you do not find fish at level D. But, as is often the case, more fish are found on the bottom (E). After working those fish, you move to a different position around the perimeter of the hole, then repeat the same procedure.

Index

Italics indicate fly patterns

Cowles Creative Publishing,
Incorporated offers a variety of
how-to-books. For information write:

Cowles Creative Publishing
Subscriber Books
5900 Green Oak Drive
Minnetonka, MN 55343

Photo Credits

Note: **T**=*Top*, **C**=*Center*, **B**=*Bottom*, **L**=*Left*, **R**=*Right*, **I**=*Inset*

©**Ted Fauceglia,**
p.38TL, p.38TR, p.39BL, p.40 *Darter, Sculpin,*
p.41TL.

©**W. D. Schmid,**
p.40 *Chub, Dace, Shiner.*

©**Jim Schollmeyer,**
p.36TL, p.36BR, p.37TR, p.37BL, p.38ML,
p.38BL, p.39TL, p.39TR, p.41BL.